FOREWORD

"Frontiers of America" dramatizes some of the explorations and discoveries of real pioneers in simple, uncluttered text. America's spirit of adventure is seen in these early people who faced dangers and hardship blazing trails, pioneering new water routes, becoming Western heroes as well as legends, and building log forts and houses as they settled in the wilderness.

Although today's explorers and adventurers face different frontiers, the drive and spirit of these early pioneers in America's past still serve as an inspiration.

ABOUT THE AUTHOR

During her years as a teacher and reading consultant in elementary schools, Mrs. McCall developed a strong interest in the people whose pioneering spirit built our nation. When she turned to writing as a full-time occupation, this interest was the basis for much of her work. She is the author of many books and articles for children and adults, and co-author of elementary school social studies textbooks.

Frontiers of America

PIONEERS on EARLY WATERWAYS

DAVY CROCKETT TO MARK TWAIN

By Edith McCall

Illustrations by Carol Rogers

CⱵ CHILDRENS PRESS, CHICAGO

Library of Congress Cataloging in
Publication Data
McCall, Edith S
    Pioneers on early waterway, Davy Crockett to
Mark Twain.
    1.   Inland water transportation—U.S.—
Juvenile literature.   2.   Frontier and pioneer
life—U.S.—Juvenile literature.
PZ7.M1229.Pi   j386   61-10104
ISBN 0-516-03357-3

New 1980 Edition
Copyright© 1961 by Regensteiner
Publishing Enterprises, Inc.
All rights reserved. Published
simultaneously in Canada.
Printed in the United States of America.

4 5 6 7 8 9 10 11 R 93 92 91

ADVENTURES ON EARLY AMERICAN WATERWAYS

DAVY CROCKETT AND THE RING-TAILED ROARER

Davy Crockett sat on the deck of a flatboat, one arm hooked over the long steering oar at the back of the boat. The boat floated slowly down the Ohio River, needing little help from the four men of the crew. Davy leaned back, resting against the forked stick that held the steering oar.

It was a lazy, quiet day, back in the time when the United States was a new country just beginning to settle the land along the Ohio River and the many rivers that fed into it. All the traveling that was done in the frontier country was by horseback over the narrow trails through the woods or by boat on the rivers. The Ohio River was the great highway to the west. It led to the Mississippi, and the boats could float all the way down to the city of New Orleans near the Gulf of Mexico.

Davy Crockett liked the life of a scout or a hunter better than the life of a boatman. But he and his friends had a load of furs and bacon, things to sell that would bring them a little money. They had put together a flatboat of rough oak boards, loaded it, and were off for New Orleans. There they would sell the furs and the bacon. Then they would pull the flatboat apart and sell the oak boards for lumber, for the box-like flatboats were too clumsy to be poled back up the rivers against the current. The flatboatmen would make their way back home on foot.

The flatboat drifted on. Davy moved the steering oar a little to head the boat around a bend. But the quiet of the summer afternoon made him sleepy and he soon settled back again. He was having trouble keeping his eyes open when he saw a keelboat pulling alongside the flatboat. There on the deck was a sight that brought Davy to his feet. A big boatman lay on the other boat deck, fast asleep. His mouth was wide open, and his snores were loud and long. It was more than Davy Crockett could stand.

"Can't let him go on like that," he muttered. "The poor man will swallow a fly!" Quickly, he lifted the long steering oar from the water. He swung it neatly over onto the deck of the keelboat and tapped it against the sleeper's head.

The whiskery boatman was on his feet before Davy could get the steering oar back into place. He rubbed his head and glared about to see what had hit him. His eyes fell on Davy, who now leaned on the steering oar as if nothing had happened.

"Hello, stranger!" the man bellowed. "Who asked you to crack my head?"

Davy grinned. He yelled back, "Didn't mind doing you the favor at all, my friend. I didn't think you wanted to sunburn your teeth."

On both boats, the other boatmen got to their feet, for they saw some fun coming. They kept the boats alongside each other to see what would happen to bring some excitement into the lazy afternoon. It was easy to see that something was about to happen, for the angry keelboatman was arching his neck and neighing like a horse. This was a sign, known to men of the rivers, that he wanted Davy Crockett to battle him in a fist fight.

Davy saw, heard and understood. He tucked his hands up under his armpits and flapped his arms as if they were wings.

"Cock-a-doodle-doo!" he crowed. This meant, in the boatmen's sign language, "I'll fight you!"

Now the keelboatman began a marching about the deck that was part of the fun. He strutted about, swelling his red-shirted chest and beating upon it with his fists. He circled about, not looking at Davy at all. Then, at last he stopped, facing the flatboat where Davy stood, arms folded on his chest. The keelboat-man spat a great "chaw" of tobacco into the river. Then he began the next step in starting a fight. He opened his mouth wide and yelled louder than an Indian on the warpath.

"YI-I-I-i-i-i! Ya-HOO! Yow-ow, OOO,-yah-hoo-OOO!" he roared. "I'm half-horse 'n' half-alligator! I'm a ring-tailed roarer and a ring-tailed screamer, too! I'm a reg'lar snapping turtle and look out for me! I can lick my weight in wildcats and swallow them whole! I can outrun, outjump and outfight any man in sight. I'll be on yer back quicker 'n greased lightnin,' and if yer a game chicken, I'll pick all the feathers off'n you! Whoop! WHOO-OOP!"

He beat on his chest again, tossed back the tangled black hair that hung down to his shoulders, and neighed again. Davy still stood on the flatboat deck, arms crossed and legs spread. He knew better than to stop the "ring-tailed roarer" in the middle of his boast. But when the last neigh died out, he also knew that it was his turn to act.

"Give us no more of your chin music!" he yelled. "Cock-a-doodle-doo! Tie up your boat and set your kickers on shore. I'll give you a licking that'll set yo're hide to stingin' and take the boastin' out of ye for good!" Davy leaped in the air and crowed again, flapping his "wings" as he did so.

The men on both boats were happy to help. They soon had the keelboat and the flatboat tied to the trunks of trees that grew along the river bank. The "ring-tailed roarer" took a cap from his head and laid it carefully on the deck. In the cap was a big red feather, the sign that he had fought and beaten every man on his boat who had cared to fight him. Then he jumped to the shore. When he got there, he limbered his legs by leaping up and down.

Davy, too, headed for the shore, as did a number of the boatmen. It was when Davy stood in front of the "half-horse, half-alligator" that he saw how really big the man was. Davy knew that he would have to be fast on his feet and duck most of the blows if he were to keep from being beaten.

Again the boatman leaped into the air. "Take care how I light on you!" he cried to Davy.

Davy did his best to take care, but the first blow

from the big man shook him so that he felt as if his insides had turned to jelly. But before the keelboatman could pull himself together for another leap, Davy was on his feet and punching hard into the man's ribs. It was like a fight between a lively dog and a clumsy, shaggy bear. Davy jumped in time after time, quickly, and as quickly backed off. But sometimes he could not back or duck in time, and he was well battered. He even lost some teeth in the fight. He saw that to win he would have to do as the dog would do to the bear,—use his teeth.

In the rivermen's fights, no holds were barred. There were no rules against biting, kicking or doing anything else that a fighter thought might help him win. Often a keelboatman had only one ear because a man he was fighting had bitten the other one off. Davy knew he could not last long enough to wear the big man down any other way, so he sank his teeth into a tender spot when he got a chance to do so, and he held on for dear life.

"Ow! OOW-ow-owoo-oo!" the ring-tailed roarer yelled. But Davy would not be shaken off. At last the flatboat crew pulled Davy away and hurried him onto the flatboat before the keelboatman could recover.

One of them untied the boat and the others took poles and shoved the boat out into the water, just as the keelboatman was about to leap on board. Davy's eyes were swollen nearly shut so that he could scarcely see, but he could make out the blurred form of the big man still leaping about on shore and could hear him roaring until the flatboat rounded a bend.

"Meanest colt I ever tried to break," he said.

Some people say that the story of Davy Crockett's fight with the keelboatman is just a tale someone made up. Others say it is true. After Davy Crockett died as a hero in the Battle of the Alamo in Texas in 1836, some papers were found which Davy was supposed to have written. The fight story was on one of those papers. It ended, "And although I didn't come out second best, I took care not to wake up a ring-tailed roarer with an oar again."

Whether or not Davy's fight really took place, it is true that there were many fights like it among the boatmen, for it was their main sport. The men who poled boats up the rivers had to be strong. They were proud to be rough and tough, and each man had to fight to prove that he was not afraid.

He had to prove that he was strong before a keelboat

owner would give him a job, for it took strong men to move the heavy, wooden boat up the river against the current. Flatboating was much easier, for there was only the downstream trip. But keelboats were built to carry goods and people up the river, too. Instead of being shaped like floating boxes, as flatboats were, keelboats were long and narrow, shaped something like a cigar. This was to make it easier to move them against the water, but still it took very strong men to fight the river currents and pull the boats from New Orleans all the way up to Pittsburgh.

There were no motors or engines to help move boats upriver in those days. The keelboats usually had tall masts, and a big square sail was sometimes opened. But the wind had to be blowing the right way for the sail to be of much help. The men poled the boat up the river when they could, and pulled it with a long rope when they couldn't pole it. There were a few oars on the boat, but they did not help much.

At New Orleans, the goods that were wanted by people on the farms and in the towns along the rivers were loaded onto the keelboats and put into the cargo box. This was a cabin that took up most of the space in the boat. When it was full, the upriver trip began.

The big, husky keelboatmen no longer could lie on the deck and sleep as Davy's ring-tailed roarer had been doing. Each man worked and worked hard all day long.

If the water was not deep, four men of the crew would line up on the running board on each side of the cargo box. This was a strip of deck with wooden cleats nailed to it to help the men in their moccasined feet keep from slipping. Each of the men faced the stern. Each had a pole about twenty feet long, called a *setting pole*. The pole's lower end was covered with iron and pointed to dig into the river bottom. The upper end was rounded and padded so that the boatman could lean hard on it with his shoulder.

When the men were ready, the steersman took his place on the roof of the cargo box near the back of the boat. It was his job to steer the boat with the long flat-ended steering oar and to keep the men at the poles working together.

"Stand to your poles!" he would cry, and the men stood ready.

"Set poles!" he called then, and each man sank his pole's end into the river bottom.

"Down on her!" was the next order, and the men

leaned into their work, walking towards the back of the boat, bending forward as they neared the end of the pole's reach. Sometimes they were in crawling position, pushing with all their strength to keep the boat moving.

The patroon, as the steersman was called, watched. At the instant the first man reached the end of his walk, the patroon called out, "Lift poles!"

Quickly, the men turned about, lifting their poles as they did so. They hurried back to their starting places, trying to get set for the next push before the current moved the boat backward.

Sometimes the bottom was too soft or the river too deep for poling. Then the men used a rope and pulled the boat from the bank. The rope was tied to the mast. From there it ran through an iron ring tied to the end of a short rope attached at the prow of the boat. One of the men would swim to the shore, or jump if the boat were near enough, carrying the end of the rope with him. The other men scrambled to the shore, too, and each took a firm grip on the rope and put it over his shoulder. They struggled along in a line, climbing over rocks, hanging onto bushes to keep from sliding into the water, slipping on muddy banks, and moving

ahead the best they could as they pulled the heavy
boat. If there was no place at all to walk, they swam.

Once in a while they used the rope in another way,
called *warping*. There were always one or two little
rowboats with the keelboat—*skiffs*, they called them.
Two or three men would get into a skiff and, taking
the rope with them, would row to a strong tree on the
bank some distance up the river. They wound the
rope around the tree and tied it firmly. The men back
on the boat then pulled hand over hand on the rope

until the boat was even with the tree. By that time, a second skiff had gone upriver with another rope which was also tied to the boat and tied it to another tree. And so the boat made its slow way up the river.

On the cargo box roof sat the luckiest man of the crew. He was the fiddler, and his work was mostly to entertain the men and set a beat for them to follow in working the poles. He squawked away at his fiddle, keeping his foot tapping. When the boat was going along, he would begin a song and the men would all join in, singing loudly while they worked. One of the favorites was *Shawneetown*.

> *Hard upon the beech oar—*
> *She moves too slow!*
> *All the way to Shawneetown,*
> *Long while ago.*
> *Some rows up, but we rows down,*
> *All the way to Shawneetown,*
> *Pull away, pull away!*

At night, the keelboat would be tied up at the bank. The cook would go ashore and build a fire to cook some salt pork with potatoes if they had them or corn cakes if they didn't. After supper and some drinks of whiskey washed down with river water, the boatmen looked for excitement. There was usually a fight then, either on the boat or in a near-by town. Sometimes they danced on the keelboat cargo-box roof. When they were tired they rolled themselves up in dirty old blankets on the shore or on the boat roof. If it rained, they huddled in the cabin with the cargo.

It was a rough life, and only rough men could take it. Roughest of them all was Mike Fink, who came to be known as King of the Keelboatmen. Mike was the greatest "ring-tailed roarer" of them all.

MIKE FINK, KING OF KEELBOATMEN

Mike Fink was born fighting, so they say. There certainly was fighting all around him, for he was born in one of the little log cabins built near Fort Pitt, on the point of land where two rivers meet to form the Ohio River. It was the place where fighting had been going on ever since the English, the French and the Indians had begun to argue over who owned the land. When Mike was born, around 1770, the land around Fort Pitt was the frontier where people had to fight to stay alive.

When he was ten, Mike learned to shoot one of the long rifles that men used in those days. A boy had to be strong to stay on his feet when he fired such a gun. And Mike grew stronger and stronger. He also became a better shot as he practiced. Soon he could outshoot every man and boy around Fort Pitt and the little town of Pittsburgh.

There were shooting matches quite often. Men paid for a chance to shoot at a target placed on a tree. There were five prizes to shoot for, the four quarters into which a steer could be cut for meat, plus the "fifth quarter," which was the hide. The hide could be sold for more than any quarter of meat was worth, and it was the first prize. Sometimes Mike bought five shots and won all five prizes. After this happened a few times, the other men gave him the "fifth quarter" free to pay him for staying out of the shooting match.

When Mike was seventeen, he became a scout. There was Indian fighting going on then, and Mike would go out with a company of soldiers to spy out the places where Indians were hiding.

The story was told that once Mike Fink found "Indian sign" and followed the trail for several days. He became hungry for fresh meat, but he knew that if he shot "Bang-all," as he called his rifle, the Indians would hear it and know he was near.

He grew very tired of eating nothing but dried corn and "jerk," as the strips of dried meat frontiersmen carried with them were called. One morning, he spied a deer feeding at the edge of the woods.

"I've just got to have some fresh meat," he thought, and crept nearer the deer. But as he raised his rifle to take aim, the thought came to him that he might not live to eat the deer meat, for he knew that he was near

the Indian camp. He did not pull the trigger.

As he stood there, he saw an Indian moving into the open space between him and the deer. The Indian, too, was out for fresh deer meat. He dropped to his knee and took aim at the deer.

Mike raised his rifle again. But this time he aimed at the Indian. At the very instant that the Indian fired and brought down the deer, old Bang-all rang out, too. It was as if one shot had been fired. The Indian fell, and Mike cut deer meat without bringing other Indians upon himself.

Stories began to be told about things the young scout did. Each person who re-told a story added a little to it. Before long, true stories were changed until they became "tall tales." Frontier people had little to do in the long winter evenings but tell each other stories. The stories about Mike Fink were told and re-told until no one knew what was true and what was a legend, especially after Mike became a keel-boatman.

A keelboat captain who needed another hand on his boat heard of the young scout.

"If he's as strong as they say he is, I can use him," the captain said.

Mike liked the idea of becoming a boatman. It meant he could see all the cities along the rivers and lead a life of adventure. Besides, there was no better way to earn money in those days than as a keelboatman. From childhood, Mike had listened to the wild wail of the wooden horns the keelboat patroons blew when they were ready to shove off from the Pittsburgh landings to start the long journey down the Ohio and the Mississippi. It had always sounded exciting to him, and soon he was learning how to handle a setting pole.

He began his work as a boatman in the days when pioneers were going down the Ohio River on flatboats or rafts, heading for the newly opened land in Ohio, Kentucky, or Indiana. Each spring as the ice broke in the rivers near Pittsburgh, the Ohio River suddenly became alive with boats. There were rafts, quickly thrown together of logs, turning about in the current as a pioneer tried to steer it with a pole. His family and all he owned in the world—perhaps a plow, his gun, a horse and a pair of chickens—would be huddled in the middle of the rocking platform.

The raft could swing alongside a fine Kentucky boat, a good, solid flatboat with a roofed-over cabin, carrying another pioneer family to a home in the west. Big boats, little boats, good ones and some that seemed ready to break apart—they made the river a busy highway.

At night, the pioneers tied their boats and visited from deck to deck, singing, dancing sometimes, and telling stories often. Sooner or later, talk would turn to stories of the kings of the river—the keelboatmen. And Mike Fink had not been a keelboatman long before the stories about him overshadowed those of other men who had worn the red feather in their caps. He became known as "The Snapping Turtle" on the Ohio, and "The Snag" on the Mississippi.

Sometimes a pioneer going west really saw the "King of the Keelboatmen." Mike had worked his way up fast and had become patroon of a keelboat in a short time. People on the flatboats saw him standing at his steering oar, shouting orders to his crew as if he were indeed a king. Some even heard him give his fighting boast, and it was something they never forgot.

"I'm a Salt River roarer!" Mike would shout as he strutted about. "I'm a ring-tailed squealer! I'm a reg'lar screamer from the old Massassip! WHOOP! I'm half wild horse and half alligator and put together with red hot snappin' turtle! I can outrun, outjump, outshoot, outbrag, outdrink, outfight any man on both sides of the river from Pittsburgh to New Orleans an' back again to St. Louis. Come on, you flatters, you bargers, you keelers! See how tough I am to chaw! I ain't had a fight for two days, and I'm spoilin' for exercise. Cock-a-doodle-doo!"

One day, so the story went, Mike's keelboat was floating lazily down the river. Mike lay on his back on the roof of the cargo box, singing loudly and just letting time pass. He turned his head and chanced to see a fine flock of sheep feeding on a grassy slope that led down to the riverbank.

"Ho, boys!" said Mike. "I see some good fresh meat for our supper. Head to and make her fast."

The crew moved the keelboat into a little cove that cut into the shoreline at the foot of the slope where the sheep were grazing. Soon the boat was tied fast.

Mike never spent money if he could get something for nothing. He had an idea as to how he could get some of those sheep without paying for them and without really stealing them. He went down into the cabin for a leather bag of snuff,—"sneezing powder," some people called it.

He went on shore, taking the snuff with him. He walked up to one of the sheep and rubbed some of the black powder onto the animal's nose and face. The sheep was soon making strange noises, rubbing its face in the grass and jumping about wildly.

"Ho, ho!" said Mike, and did the same to five more sheep.

When the six animals were acting as if they were going mad, Mike sent a couple of men up to the cabin where the shepherd lived.

"Tell him he had better come down here and see what is wrong with his sheep," Mike said, and laughed loudly.

The boatmen hurried up to the cabin. Soon they were back with the man who owned the sheep. He looked very worried when he saw the strange way in which the six sheep were acting.

"What is wrong with them?" he asked Mike.

Mike looked very sad. "You don't know?" he asked gently.

"No, I don't know," said the farmer.

Mike looked about as if he were afraid someone might hear what he was about to say. He crooked his finger for the farmer to come close.

"Did you ever hear of the black murrain?" he half whispered.

"Can't say as I did," said the farmer.

Mike shook his head. "A terrible sickness. And once it starts in a flock, it spreads fast. All the sheep up the river has it. Dying by the hundreds."

"You don't say!" said the farmer. He began to look worried. "Is there no cure for it?"

Mike's face was even longer than before. "None. None but shootin' them as has it before it spreads to the others."

The farmer looked up at his flock. The animals were close together, with the six strange acting ones mixed in with the others.

"Why, I'd kill the good ones if I tried to shoot the sick ones," he said. "No man could single out those six and miss the others!"

Mike straightened his shoulders and stood tall. "No man?" he said, and his voice was proud. "No man, you say? How about Mike Fink?"

There wasn't a man along the rivers who didn't know that Mike Fink could shoot a tin cup off a man's head at a hundred feet and never move a hair of the man's head.

"Mike Fink, yes. But no one else!"

Mike said, "Then you are in luck, manny. *I* am Mike Fink."

It took the farmer a moment to get over the shock of facing up to the great Snapping Turtle. Then he begged, "Shoot them for me before the others catch it!"

But Mike shook his head. "Maybe I hadn't better. Maybe they'll get well."

The poor farmer imagined he could see signs of the illness on the faces of his other sheep.

"Please, Captain Fink, please shoot them and roll them into the river before all my sheep get the black murrain!"

"Well, manny, I don't think I should, just on my own say-so that it's the black murrain. Maybe you'd better go ask the neighbors."

One of the sheep snorted terribly just then. The farmer said, "No, no! I'll take your word for it. Captain Fink, I'll give you two gallons of my best peach brandy if you'll shoot them for me."

Mike acted as if he were thinking very hard, fighting to let himself agree to shoot the sheep. Finally he said, "Yes, manny, I'll do it for you. Go and get the peach brandy."

The farmer hurried away. Soon he was back with two jugs, and the boatmen put them into the boat. Mike took his rifle and carefully aimed at one of the strange acting sheep.

"Bang!" The black-faced sheep fell and the others scattered.

"Bang!" and another was down. Mike shot four times more, and the six sheep lay dead. The boatmen rolled each of them into the river.

Mike turned to the farmer. "They're all taken care of, manny."

"Oh, thank you, thank you, Captain Fink," the farmer said. He went into his flock, searching for signs of the black murrain on the faces of his other sheep. Of course there were none, and at last he went back to his cabin. By that time, it was growing dark, and it seemed only natural for the keelboat to stay tied to the bank at the foot of the hill.

During the night, Mike had his men jump into the water and haul the six sheep aboard the keelboat. At dawn they moved on, well supplied with meat. The keelboatmen thought it was a great joke, never once thinking about whether or not their hero had been very honest.

On down the Ohio went the keelboat, and almost everywhere it stopped some story grew about what Mike Fink had done. But even Mike's crew usually went right on past a place at the southern edge of what is now Illinois, called Cave-in-Rock. There was a great dark hole in the stone face of a bluff there, and pirates lived in the cave. They sent terror all along the river with their murders and robberies of those who stopped too near. The legend grew that Mike Fink was the one who finally cleaned out the cave of the robbers, but there was no proof of this.

Mike was "King of the Keelboatmen" until he left the rivers to go to the far west with the fur trappers. But by that time, a great change had come to the rivers, and the keelboatmen were no longer kings of the river. The first steamboats were chugging, puffing and snorting their way up and down the Ohio and the lower Mississippi. The days of the ring-tailed roarers were ending.

MRS. TROLLOPE'S
TRIP TO MEMPHIS

The city of New Orleans was already very old on New Year's Day in 1828, but to the lady who made her way to the river front that day it seemed raw and new and strange. For she had come from England, where the cities were old when Columbus sailed west.

Carefully, holding her long skirts close to keep them from touching the mud and the boxes and bales that were all about, the lady picked her way towards a clumsy-looking boat with a plank leading from the wharf to its lower deck. Behind her came two girls, each dressed like her mother in a dark woolen coat and long dress. A sixteen-year-old boy followed them, carrying some of their luggage.

"On which ship do we sail, Mother?" the boy asked.

"Henry, I am told it is not to be called a ship, but a steamboat. It is that one directly ahead of us." The lady, whose name was Mrs. Trollope, nodded her head in the direction of a steamboat with the name *Belvidere* painted on the wooden covers over the side paddle wheels. Of the several steamboats docked at

New Orleans that day, the *Belvidere* was not the largest nor was it the finest. But it would become the best known, because Mrs. Trollope was keeping notes of her travels for a book that would be published after she went back to England.

There were not so many boats at the river front that New Year's Day as there usually were, because it was winter. A few months earlier there had been dozens of flatboats tied up, waiting to be unloaded. Some had brought furs loaded onto them at St. Louis or up the Missouri River. Others had brought barrels and barrels of pork from Ohio. From all the farmlands they had brought flour and whiskey to be loaded onto the tall-masted sailing ships that would take the goods from New Orleans to the eastern cities of the United States or even to Europe.

There were a few keelboats being loaded with goods the sailing ships had brought to New Orleans. They would go up to the river cities of Natchez, Memphis and St. Louis on the Mississippi and Louisville and Cincinnati on the Ohio. Later there would be loads of trading goods for the St. Louis fur trade, and goods for the places that were ice-bound in winter. But more and more, steamboats were taking the place of keelboats, for they could go up the river faster than the boatmen could pull or pole the keelboats.

Mrs. Trollope stopped at the beginning of the plank that led from the dock to the *Belvidere*. She turned about to see that everyone was ready to go on board.

"Cecilia, Emily—mind your step, now," she said to the two girls. Cecilia was eleven and Emily was nine years old. "Henry, don't try to carry too much."

Henry was as tall as a man, but he had been sick a great deal and was not as strong as he looked. Yet he hated to have his mother fussing over him. He looked about to see if anyone heard before he answered, "Yes, Mother."

Behind Henry came a man who was a servant of the Trollope family. He was heavily loaded with luggage. His neat gray and black striped trousers were splashed with mud, but he did not complain. Two more people were with the Trollope family, another lady named Miss Wright, and a young man who was looking about as if he wanted to remember everything he saw. And that is just what he was doing, for he was an artist. The pictures he drew of the *Belvidere* helped make it famous.

Mrs. Trollope turned and walked out on the plank,

her eyes straight ahead. A group of whiskered men, with more dirt than a few splashes of mud on their trousers, stared as the people from England walked onto the steamboat.

One of the men spit out some chewing tobacco onto the deck and Mrs. Trollope pulled her skirt closer. There seemed to be no other women about.

Cecilia pulled at her mother's sleeve. "Mother," she whispered, "are we the only girls on this ship?"

"Steamboat, dear—not ship. I will ask the clerk."

Mrs. Trollope spoke to the steamboat man who was leading them to the ladies' cabin. "Yes, madam, you and your party are the only ladies on the *Belvidere* this trip. But you will be comfortable, I am sure."

When Mrs. Trollope saw the tiny cabin with its bunk beds like narrow shelves on two walls, she was glad that there would be only four people in it. It was at the stern of the boat, and little light came in through the two small windows. There was a fine carpet on the floor and a few good chairs. Curtains hung in front of the sleeping bunks. But everything in the cabin showed the dirt of the three years that the *Belvidere* had been going up and down the rivers.

"This is the ladies' washroom, madam," the clerk

said. He opened a door into a tiny room. It had a table on which were a pitcher of river water and a tin basin. On the wall was a roller towel. The clerk closed the door and bowed to the ladies.

"Dinner will be served at noon in the gentlemen's cabin," he said. "I trust you will find everything satisfactory."

As he left them, the women and the girls looked at each other a little sadly. Then Mrs. Trollope shrugged her shoulders. "Ah, well," she said, "we can't hope for everything to be as fine in so new a country as it is in old England."

Emily said, "Are there ships like this in England, Mother?"

"Steamboats, dear. No, not like this. The English steamers do not have two decks, like a two-story building, as this one has."

Miss Wright had been to America before. She explained to the girls, "The English do not need to travel in steamboats as the Americans do, girls. England has no wilderness without roads as America has. Stagecoaches can take you almost anywhere in England, but in America there are only a few stage-coach roads west of the Appalachian Mountains. The rivers are the roads, and so most people travel by steamboat. Why, the whole of England is little longer from south to north than is the distance from New Orleans to Memphis, where we shall leave the *Belvidere.*"

"And it is another thousand miles by river to Cincinnati, Ohio, where we shall be going after we leave Memphis," Mrs. Trollope said. "It is hard to realize what a great wilderness the Americans have set out to tame."

Just then there was a great banging and a pounding. The whole boat began to shake. "Oh, mama, what is that?" Emily cried.

Mrs. Trollope looked as frightened as the girls, but Miss Wright laughed. "It is only the steam engines beginning to work," she explained. "It is a good thing that I have been on an American steamboat before or, I declare, you would be like lost babes. Our journey has begun. Can't you feel the motion? Come, let us go out onto the deck."

The two ladies and the girls left the cabin. Henry and Mr. Hervieu, the artist, came out of the gentlemen's cabin about the same time. They all took places near the rail to watch as the buildings of New Orleans grew smaller. The noise of the steam engines and the splashing of water in the turning paddle wheels made it hard to hear anything else, but now and then the sound of men's voices drifted down from over the travelers' heads.

Henry leaned outward and looked up. He could see that the deck above the cabins was roofed over but open, like a porch. At its rails leaned dozens of men.

"They all seem to look alike," Henry said. "Who are they?"

Miss Wright said, "They are mostly Kentucky flatboatmen. They brought their flatboats down to New Orleans, sold their goods and the boats and are going back home by steamboat. They can travel for very little money up on that deck. They bring their own food, and they help load wood onto the boat. Of course, they have to sleep the best they can on the deck. They have no cabins."

Henry wanted to see how the men got up there. He made his way through passages that led to the bow of the boat. He passed the big square wooden covers over the paddle wheels, the piles of cordwood that the steamboatmen were feeding into the furnaces, and the machinery that turned the paddle wheels. On the forward deck were boxes and barrels of cargo. Up near the boat's prow he saw a ladder-like stairway leading up to the upper deck.

For a moment, Henry thought he would like to go up the ladder. But a hand on his elbow stopped him, and he heard the voice of the man servant who was traveling with the Trollopes.

"I wouldn't go up there, Master Henry. They are a rough lot of fellows and likely to make sport of a young gentleman like you."

Henry looked up at the "rough lot of fellows." They were dressed in the buckskins and coarse cloth trousers and shirts of the frontier, and most of them had rough beards.

Henry stepped back from the ladder rails. He said, "I wonder why so many of them have red whiskers?"

The man-servant smiled. "They are indeed a red-bearded lot, Master Henry. Perhaps they are a bit of Ireland moved to America."

Henry knew that he and Mr. Hervieu would have bunks in the gentlemen's cabin, but he wondered where the servant was to sleep. He would be in for more "roughing up" than Henry if he were to try to mix with the Kentuckians.

"The clerk was kind enough to give me a place with the crew," the servant explained.

Henry, seeing the stares of the frontiersmen at his English clothes, felt uncomfortable. He went back to join his family. By this time they had all found chairs and were sitting outside the cabins. It was a pleasant, sunny day. Henry, too, found a chair and sat down to watch the wooded shoreline go by.

They were all beginning to feel a little sleepy in the warm sunshine when something happened to make them wide awake. The *Belvidere's* engines slowed and she nosed in toward the shoreline. A long pile of firewood was stacked near the shore, and the wood-seller's cabin was just beyond.

The mate's voice rang out in a kind of sing-song.

Wood-pile, wood-pile!

Where are the wooders?

There was no time to wonder where the wooders were. Down they came from the upper deck. The gangplank was scarcely in place before the first bearded frontiersman was out on it. They whooped and hollered loudly enough to wake every sleeping creature for miles and miles. Some even played a game of leap-frog, flying over each other's heads and backs to the long woodpile. There each man loaded his arms with pine logs and, quieted down a bit, carried wood onto the steamboat.

The wood-stop excitement was hardly over when the ringing of a gong told the Trollopes that dinner time had come. They all went into the gentlemen's cabin. Like the ladies' cabin, it had bunk beds along the walls, but many more of them. Down the center of the long room, tables were laid. The Trollopes took seats and were introduced to the gentlemen sitting near by. All the men seemed to be called "General," "Colonel," or "Major," although they did not wear army uniforms.

"Were all Americans army officers?" Mrs. Trollope asked when she could.

"In the Indian fighting and in the War of 1812, there were many small companies formed in the west," she was told. "Most of the gentlemen of the type who would be paying passengers on this steamboat were officers, even if only for a few weeks. They like to use the titles."

Waiters brought in plates and platters of food which were quickly passed from person to person. The men all heaped their plates high with food. There were

beefsteaks, baked ham, and roast turkey and duck, and cold sliced meat, too. Then came potatoes, rice and corn.

"We will have some pleasant talk now," Mrs. Trollope thought.

But she was wrong. All the gentlemen were much too busy stuffing themselves with food. No one talked. As soon as the dessert tarts had been served, the ladies and girls went to the ladies' cabin to rest and recover from the shock of their first meal on the boat.

Mrs. Trollope said, "Did you see those men eating with their knives? I thought they'd swallow blade and all!"

Miss Wright said, "And the way they pick their teeth with their knives, right at table!"

"I could live through mealtimes, if only they wouldn't chew tobacco and spit," Mrs. Trollope groaned. "And they call them 'gentlemen'!"

The supper hour was like dinner except there was only meat and bread. In the morning, after a restless night in the bunks, the Trollopes were fed whatever was left from last night's supper.

The *Belvidere* moved slowly up the Mississippi, mile after mile. The first city they reached was

Natchez. They could see the old settlement down on the river's level, and the newer, finer buildings high on the bluff above the river. That night the sky was bright with the glow of a forest fire. But most interesting to the people from England were the alligators which lay sleepily at the river's edge, looking for all the world like logs. "Crocodiles," Mrs. Trollope called them, not knowing of the difference between American alligators and the meat-eating African crocodiles.

"Have they ever been known to eat anyone?" she asked one of the gentlemen passengers. The gentleman was bored with the long hours of riding and saw a chance to have some fun.

"It's too horrible to talk about, ma'am," he said. "But yes, them crockydiles has been known to eat people. Why, one of them ate a man and his wife and their five children all in one night. Feller about like that woodcutter we jest saw."

He glanced at the faces of the Trollopes. Emily's eyes were so wide with horror that he decided to tell a gentler tale to while away the time. Soon he was off on a story about an Indian fur trader who came down the Mississippi with a load of furs in his canoe. When he was about a day's trip above New Orleans, the Indian saw a bear on the shore and decided to shoot him.

"Bang went his gun!" the story-teller said. He saw that all the Trollopes were hanging on his words and interrupted his story to ask, "Have you ever seen an injun?"

Mrs. Trollope said, "No, we haven't, but Indians are one of the sights we hope to see while in America."

"Indeed," said the gentleman. "Well, now, this here injun hadn't never missed his shot before, but he did this time. Yes, ma'am. He looked at that b'ar, and that b'ar looked right back at him. 'Course the injun's gun was empty, so he couldn't shoot again. 'I'm gettin' out of here!' he yelled, for he saw that the bear was so angry he was gettin' set to spring right into the canoe. So at the very instant the bear went flying through the air, the injun was flyin' towards the bank. The bear landed in the canoe so hard it sent the boat scootin' down the river, furs, supplies and all, with the bear a-settin' where the injun had been." The story-teller cast an eye in Mrs. Trollope's direction.

"Indeed!" she said. "Go on."

"Yes, sir—ma'am, I mean, begging your pardon. Well, by'n'by that canoe got down to New Orleans. Folks watchin' from the banks and from the other boats thought it was some new kind of injun that wore a heavy fur coat." He looked at Mrs. Trollope again, and then went on.

"One feller that had been to your country said he was sure it was an Englishman in a driving coat." He waited for the English people's laugh before he went on.

"Well, sir—ma'am—that bear was about to go right on down to the Gulf of Mexico when someone threw a fishline out, hooked onto the canoe and pulled him to the dock. You know what that bear did then?"

Emily's eyes were wide. Cecilia and Henry looked as if they expected almost anything to happen, and even Mrs. Trollope seemed to be hanging on every word.

"He set foot on land, gave a terrific growl that blasted open a path in front of him and leaped to the woods in three leaps. That was the last they ever saw of him, although there are some as says there's a fur trader comes often that looks a lot like him." Just then the dinner gong rang and the storyteller was gone.

Even the stories ran out by the end of the fifth day. The boat traveled only in the daytime, and it took a long time to go four hundred miles up the Mississippi. The Trollopes learned to watch, as the pilot did, for sand bars on which the boat might get stuck, and for the trees half hidden by the water. They learned that the ones that lie still, waiting to catch a boat, are called *snags*. Those that rock up and down are *sawyers*.

Early in the morning of the day they should have reached Memphis there was a sudden bump that almost threw them out of the bunks. They could feel the boat swinging sideways instead of going forward.

The Trollopes dressed as quickly as they could. They could hear the paddle wheels churning as the engine worked to turn them backward. As they hurried out to the deck they heard voices calling in excitement.

"It's a sawyer!" someone cried.

"No, it's a snag. We've hit a snag!"

Then the captain's voice settled the matter. "We are aground, gentlemen. We have struck a sand bar, and we are hung up nicely."

"Aground? Good heavens, how long shall we stay here?"

"Long enough to try my patience, I expect," the captain said.

It tried not only his patience but that of all the passengers as well. Breakfast, dinner and supper were eaten, and the boat had not backed off an inch. Some steamboats passed by, and a few even tried to pull the *Belvidere* free. But none could do it.

A night passed, and another breakfast and a dinner were eaten. The Trollopes knew every inch of the river bank by heart as far as they could see in each direction. Then from the upper deck there arose a great cheer, for the deck passengers had sighted a great monster of a steamboat coming towards the *Belvidere*. From its deck reached out a pair of long bars with iron hooks on the ends.

"Grappling irons," one of the men explained to Henry. Soon the steamboat had moved about to the right spot and the irons were hooked onto the *Belvidere*. The steamboat began to slowly back away.

"She's afloat! Hurray!" the cry arose. The irons were unhooked, the rescue boat backed clear, and once more the journey to Memphis could go on.

Rain began to fall as the *Belvidere* moved upriver again. Darkness came, but the captain kept the steamboat moving on toward Memphis. When it seemed the blackest and wettest of all, the *Belvidere* tied up

at the dock.

"Memphis!"

And so, into the mud and the blackness, with only a pin point of light cutting into the rain from a dim lantern, the travelers made their way to the hotel, a little wiser in the ways of travel in America.

JIM GARFIELD, CANALBOATMAN

So many settlers poured into the Ohio Valley and the lands farther west that the land away from the rivers began to fill up, too. Something had to be done to make it possible to carry goods to the farmers and to take their farm products to market.

Just a few years before Mrs. Trollope learned about steamboat travel in America, some government leaders had a meeting in New York about the problem. When they had talked it over, they said, "Canals are the answer. Road building is slow and expensive. As for railroads, they will never amount to anything. But we have canals here to connect our eastern cities. Why not dig canals in the west?"

The work started, and the big Erie Canal was dug. It reached from the Hudson River in New York to Lake Erie at the city of Buffalo. When it opened, there was a big celebration, for boats could then go from the Great Lakes to New York City. The next step was to connect the Great Lakes with the Ohio River and the Mississippi. Soon there was a network of canals.

Canalboats carried tons and tons of farm products to market, and gave the people a new way to travel, too. The cities grew even faster.

Not far from Cleveland, Ohio, where the canals from the Ohio River reached Lake Erie, a boy named James Garfield was growing up on a farm. Jim decided, when he was about thirteen years old, that he would be a sailor and see the world.

When he was fifteen, he got work as a wood-chopper on the shore of Lake Erie. Sometimes he would stop his work to watch one of the sailing ships go by on the lake. Or he would see a lake steamer puffing its way from one of the lake-shore cities to another.

"This wood chopping is not for me," he told the men he was working with. "I'm going to be a sailor. A Lake Erie boat will do for a start, and then I'll go on to the high seas."

The next spring, in 1847, Jim Garfield walked the seventeen miles from his farm home to Cleveland. His mother had not wanted him to do it, but he was about to become a sailor. He went right to the lake front where a sailing ship was tied. He walked up the gang-plank and went on board.

"Need a hand?" he asked the first sailor he saw.

"Ask the captain," said the sailor. "Here he comes now. You can hear him yourself without half tryin'."

Jim had always thought of ship's captains as big, handsome men with kind hearts. He could hardly believe that the rough voice he heard, swearing at the sailors, was that of the captain. A mean-looking man in dirty clothes came around the end of the cabin. Jim forced himself to speak up.

"Captain, do you need a hand?" he asked.

The captain looked him over, from head to foot.

"Let a landlubber like you work on my ship?" he said. "Not on your worthless life! Get off my ship before I kick you off!"

Jim left gladly. He sat down on a pile of wood on the wharf and pulled out the sandwich his mother had packed into his bundle of belongings before he left home.

"How did he know I was a landlubber?" Jim wondered. His clothes were of the kind a frontier country boy wore. Perhaps that was what gave him away. But there was nothing he could do about his clothes, for he had no money to buy sailor's clothes.

He got up and walked along the wharf, trying to get up courage to try another of the lake ships. He walked towards the place where the Ohio Canal connected with Lake Erie. There were quite a few canalboats there. A few were the packets, long and quite slender, with a sleeping and dining cabin taking up most of the length of the boat. Jim had seen the inside of one once. The walls were covered with shelf-like bunk beds, as many as four high. The dining tables filled up all the rest of the space.

But most of the canalboats waiting at the docks were freight boats, ready to carry freight from the Erie Canal or from any of the cities of the Great Lakes south through the canals to the Ohio River cities or even down to New Orleans. Many of them had long open cargo boxes, with just a small closed cabin at one end.

Jim saw a lake ship unloading copper ore into one of the open canal freight boats. He walked nearer, to see better and for something to do while he decided on his next step.

"Jim! Jim Garfield!"

Jim turned. There was his cousin, Amos Letcher, on the deck of one of the boats. Amos was a few years older than Jim, but he and Jim had always been good friends. Jim hurried over.

"How come you to be here, Jim?" Amos asked.

Jim said, "I'm looking for work. I came to ship as a sailor."

"Any luck yet?"

Jim shook his head. "No. I guess the captains can see I'm not a sailor, and they don't want green hands."

"How about trying a canalboat for a start?" Amos asked.

Jim thought a moment. Then he said, "Well, Amos, it's not like the high seas, but maybe it would help me get ready to be a real sailor. Is another hand needed on this boat?"

"Sure thing," said Amos. "We need another driver."

Jim brightened. He knew what a driver was. The canalboats were pulled through the canals by mules or horses walking on a specially built walk at the canal's edge called a towpath. A driver either walked behind the animals or rode on the back of one of them, driving them along the towpath.

"I could be a driver, Amos," Jim said. "I've been driving mules and horses all my life on the farm, and it shouldn't be much different on a towpath. Where's the captain?"

"You're talking to him now, Jim," Amos said, and

56

he stood taller, proud of his position.

Jim stared. Amos took on new importance in his eyes. "Are you really the canalboat captain, Amos?"

"Sure thing," Amos said. "I worked my way up to it from the job of driver. Maybe you can do the same thing."

But Jim had not yet given up his dream of the high seas. "I'll not stay on the canals that long, Amos, but I would like to start here if you'll have me."

"Come on board," said Amos. "You are hired. I'll show you your bunk, and then you can help with the loading. Pay is twelve dollars a month."

Amos introduced Jim to the five other men on the boat. All of them were older than Jim and bigger. He showed Jim the shelf that was his bed in the tiny cabin.

The only beautiful thing about the boat was its name. It was called the *Evening Star*. Soon the *Evening Star* was taking its turn at being loaded with copper ore from the big lake ship that had brought the ore from Lake Superior's shores. It was to go to Pittsburgh where there were now many factories and mills.

When the time came for the *Evening Star* to begin its journey, Jim watched the other driver for a while to see how he handled the mules on the towpath.

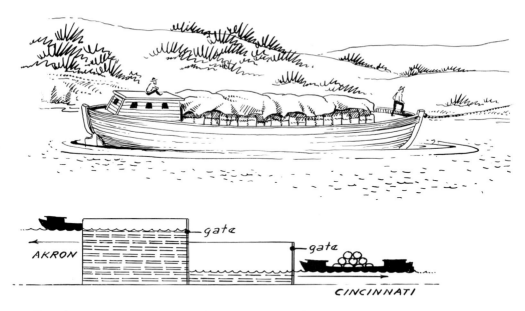

AKRON   gate   gate   CINCINNATI

Darkness came, and a lantern was lighted on the prow of the canalboat. Its beams did not cut through the blackness very far, but the boat kept on moving along slowly.

"Get some sleep, Jim," Amos said. "You go on duty at sunrise."

The boat was moving southward toward the city of Akron, which was quite a bit higher than Cleveland. To climb the hills, the canalboats had to go through locks, each one a step higher than the one before. The canals were built so that the water did not flow as the water of a river did. A long, level ditch about four

feet deep and forty feet wide was dug. When a lock
was needed, it was built with high sides and a gate at
each end.

Jim came out on deck just as the *Evening Star* was
going through the first lock. The north gate was open
and the boat floated into the lock. Then the gate was
closed behind it. The south gate was opened, and
water ran down into the lock, floating the boat higher
as the lock filled. When it was up to the level of the
next stretch of canal, the *Evening Star* left the lock and
went on its way.

Amos gave Jim a few last words of warning while

Jim was harnessing his mules, one behind the other, on the *Evening Star's* deck.

"Watch your lines, Jim. The bowline mustn't get too slack, or there could be trouble. If you meet another canalboat, be careful how you cross lines as you pass each other."

Jim felt sure he could handle the work. It looked easy. All he had to do was to walk along behind the second mule.

The bowman snubbed up the bowline on a post set at the canal's edge to help the boatmen stop the canalboats. The mule team that had been working came onto the deck to rest. Jim drove his team from the deck to the towpath and fastened the buckle at the end of the towline to the harness. The bowman loosened the line and soon the boat was moving smoothly forward, a mile and a half to two miles an hour.

"Nothing to it," thought Jim when he had covered a mile. By the end of the next mile, he was wondering how this was ever going to make a sailor of him. Just then he heard a call from Amos on the boat.

"Careful, Jim! Another boat is heading this way. Steady!"

Jim peered ahead and saw the other mule team

walking toward his on the narrow towpath. By moving to the right, he could make room enough for his animals to pass the others. The bowmen and steersmen on the boats would take care to hold one boat close to the towpath side while the other passed on the far side of the canal. But Jim was not sure how to handle the lines as the teams passed.

The other team reached his. Jim tried lifting his line for the animals to go under it, but somehow it didn't work out. He and the other driver got their lines crossed. It took only a moment to untangle them and for the second driver to move on. But Jim was not ready soon enough to start his team forward. Of course the *Evening Star* had kept on floating forward while the team stood still.

"Whip up your team, Jim, or the line will catch on that bridge," the steersman called.

"Ay, ay!" said Jim and whipped the mules to a trot.

Captain Amos saw that there was too much speed too suddenly.

"Steady, Jim!" he called. But he was too late. The lines had fallen loosely into the water. Now, suddenly, the slack was taken up and the seventy ton load of the canalboat, which had slowed almost to a stop, was a strong pull.

"Help!" yelled Jim, for he found himself, harness, mules and all, falling into the canal.

The bowman yelled, "Hold on, Jim!" and set to work to snub the line. The other crewmen who were not in their bunks sleeping jumped to the towpath to help rescue team and driver.

Jim was no swimmer, and it was lucky that the canal was only four feet deep. He got clear of the kicking, struggling animals and onto his own feet. Then he took hold of the bridle of the lead mule to steady it and lead the team back to the towpath, up the slippery, slanting mud banks. It took all the men to get things back to rights, and the men worked together quietly.

But once all were safe and ready to go again, the quiet ended. The men laughed as if they'd split their sides. Jim's face was red and he felt foolish. But he grinned in answer to the jokes the men called out.

"What did you think you were doin' down there, Jim?" Amos asked.

"Just taking my morning bath," Jim answered, and the men laughed louder than ever. The joking and teasing went on for a long time, but Jim laughed at

himself along with the others. They soon saw that he could take a joke, even when it meant a bad time for himself. He began to earn his place on the crew. He fell into the canal about once a week all through that summer, and the men enjoyed each fall more than the one before.

The *Evening Star* made its slow way through each of the twenty-one locks uphill to Akron. There it left the Ohio Canal to turn eastward into the Ohio and Pennsylvania Canal. This canal would take it to Beaver River, which flowed into the Ohio River not far below Pittsburgh. A steam tug would tow the boats through the rivers where there were no towpaths to follow.

By the time the canalboat reached the rivers, Jim was beginning to feel like an old hand on the towpath. The crewmen treated him like one of themselves except for one thing. They seemed to think he should get into a fist fight to prove how strong he was, a carry-over from the days of the "ring-tailed roarers." But Jim always talked his way out of a fight.

One day, one of the men, a big man named Murphy, said, "Are you afraid to fight, Jim?"

"No, I'm not afraid," Jim said. "But I won't fight

unless I'm in the right. When I'm wrong, I'll say I'm sorry and not fight over it."

"Hm-mm-ph," said Murphy. It was plain to see that he thought Jim a coward. No other canalboatman seemed to need any excuse at all for a fight.

Jim's test came on the day that the steam tug was being hooked on to tow the *Evening Star*. Jim was on deck, leaning on a setting pole to help get the canal-boat into position. A sailor on the steamboat threw the heavy towline towards the canalboat. Jim tried to catch it, but the boat lurched suddenly. The rope flew past him towards Murphy.

"Look out, Murphy!" Jim cried, but too late, for the rope neatly flicked Murphy's hat from his head and sent it flying into the river.

Murphy's old hat was his pride. He wore a red feather in it, just as Mike Fink did in keelboat days. His face turned purple with anger as he turned to Jim.

"What did ye do that fer?" he bellowed.

"I'm sorry, Murphy," Jim said. "It was an accident."

Murphy shouted, "I'll make ye sorry!"

He bent over and charged toward Jim like an angry bull. But Jim saw him coming and jumped quickly to one side. Murphy plunged on into the pile of copper ore in the cargo box.

"Arrr-rrrgh!" he snarled, too angry to speak.

Jim saw that he was trying to get up, and he had no wish to be pounded by Murphy's fists. So as soon as Murphy was halfway to his feet, Jim pushed him back again and held him down.

"Give it to him, Jim!" yelled Amos.

Jim went on holding Murphy down, but he did not strike him. He shook his head and said, "No. Not while he's down, Amos."

The whole crew of the canalboat and several steamboatmen gathered to watch. Murphy struggled to get up, but each time he tried, Jim pushed him back. He tried to shake Jim off, but Jim held on grimly. He was light in weight but stronger than he looked, for he had worked at wood chopping and carpenter work since he was ten years old. His arms and shoulders were strong enough to push the big man back again and again.

"Had enough?" he finally asked.

Murphy grunted.

"Am I a coward?" Jim asked.

Again Murphy grunted.

"Say I'm not a coward. Say it loud," Jim ordered.

"You're not a coward," Murphy said. Slowly, Jim let go and arose. Murphy got to his feet.

From then on, Jim was no longer looked upon as a "greenhorn landlubber." He had won his place as a member of the crew. When Amos' bowman left the *Evening Star,* Jim was given his job. His pay went up to eighteen dollars a month.

But he still went on falling into the canal. On his last trip, he nearly lost his life. It was a windy, rainy night, black as the piles of coal Jim had seen in Pittsburgh. Jim had been sleeping in the cabin when Amos called that it was time to go on duty. He was very tired, and his eyes were hardly open when he staggered out onto the wet deck.

The boat seemed to be moving along smoothly, in one of the long stretches between locks on the Ohio and Pennsylvania Canal, east of Akron. The boat's headlight lantern flickered in the wind, and scarcely cut through the rain at all.

Suddenly, Jim realized that he was very close to a lock. He reached for the towline to pull it to steady the boat and guide it into the lock. But the rope caught in the posts at the lock's edge and tightened.

Jim pulled, trying to loosen it before it should send mules and driver into the water in the night's blackness. The rope would not come loose. With all his strength, Jim tugged at it.

When it gave, it did so suddenly. Jim backed off, but he could not get his balance. Backward he went, off the wet deck into the deepening water of the lock. He lost his grip on the rope as he hit the water.

"Help!" he yelled. But his voice seemed to bound back into his own face. No one was on deck. The driver was too far ahead to hear his call on that rainy night.

Desperately, Jim clawed for the boat's side. He could not find it. He knew he was going down, sliding away into the depths of the lock and all was lost. Then, as he struggled to come up his hand touched something.

The towline! He tightened his grip and pulled himself toward the boat. It held and he made his way to the boat, where the rope was firmly caught between two of the boards that edged the deck. Jim pulled himself onto the deck and guided the rope back onto the capstan at the canalboat's prow. Then, as he sat there shivering in the blackness, peering ahead to see where the boat was going, Jim did some thinking.

He was not of the same breed as the other canalboat-men. Amos was the only one who was at all interested in books and the kind of talk Jim liked, and Jim already knew much more than Amos did. He had heard that the lake sailors were even a rougher lot than the canalboatmen. Remembering the curses of the captain of the lake ship when he had asked for work, Jim believed this to be so.

"I'm not cut out to be a sailor at all," he decided. "Maybe I was saved from drowning tonight so that I could be something else."

That was Jim's last trip as a canalboat sailor or any other kind of sailor. He decided to go to college and study. He became a teacher and then went into poli-tics. When he died, he was far, far from the life of a sailor. James Abram Garfield had become President of the United States of America.

RALPH KEELER, CABIN BOY

When Jim Garfield looked out over the waters of Lake Erie and watched the lake steamers, he might have seen one with a big sheet iron Indian, crouched on one knee and aiming an arrow out over the lake, fastened to the smokestack. It would have been the steamer *Indiana*. Jim might even have seen a nine year old boy on the deck. The boy was enjoying his first boat trip. Like Jim, he was deciding he would be a sailor.

Two years later, that boy stood on the dock at Buffalo. Just as Jim Garfield had done, he was choosing a lake boat on which to become a sailor. But Ralph Keeler was not only a "landlubber," he was also even younger and smaller than Jim.

As Ralph stood there looking over the boats, he remembered his ride on the *Indiana*. His mother and father had died not long before, and the boy was being sent from his home in Toledo, Ohio, to live with relatives in Buffalo, New York. He had loved that trip, for the waters of Lake Erie had lapped gently at the

Indiana's sides through days of watching the sailors work and hearing the clanging, hissing engines. It was then that Ralph decided to be a sailor.

Now he was eleven and a half years old. He had not been happy with his relatives in Buffalo.

"They hate me," Ralph told his friends.

"Why don't you run away?" one of the boys asked. "I'll help you."

It seemed a good idea to Ralph. His helpful friend hid him in his father's barn, enjoying having a secret. The boy brought food to Ralph, but all he could take away without being noticed was bread with lots of butter on it. To hide the bread, he put it into his trouser pockets.

After a day or two, Ralph became tired of bread and butter, especially when he had to pick pocket lint off it before he could eat it.

"I think I'll get a job on a lake steamer," he told his friend.

By this time, the friend was finding it hard to explain to his parents why he was suddenly eating so much bread and butter, and why there were so many grease spots on his trousers. He was glad to hear that he was going to lose his secret visitor. He dug into his pocket and brought out his entire fortune—five well-buttered pennies.

"That's a bully idea, Ralph," he said. "Here, take this money to help you until you can earn more. Pay me back when you have made your fortune."

He hurried off to school, and Ralph headed for the dock. He looked over the steamers tied there. He chose the finest looking one and walked to its gang-plank.

One of the sailors stopped him as he reached the deck.

"Show me to the captain's quarters," Ralph said in his most grown-up voice.

The sailor looked a bit surprised. "And, what would you be seeing the captain for, young man?" he asked.

"I wish to offer my services on board this steamer," Ralph said.

The sailor eyed him from head to foot. There wasn't much to see, for Ralph was not very tall. There was hay in his uncombed hair and bits of it clung to his wrinkled school suit. Dark streaks were on his trousers where he had wiped his buttery fingers.

"The likes of you?" the sailor asked. "And what do you think you can do on a fine lake steamer?"

"I am an experienced sailor," Ralph said, hoping the man wouldn't ask him what kind of experience he had had. Being a passenger on one journey might not seem like sailing experience to anyone but Ralph.

Just then the steward came along.

"Who is this lad?" he asked.

"Thinks he's a sailor and wants to see the captain," said the sailor. He turned and walked away.

"I take care of the hiring, boy," said the steward. "You are much too small to work on a steamer. You should be in school."

Ralph drew himself up as tall as he could. "I am self supporting," he said. He fingered the five buttery pennies in his pocket.

"How old are you?" the steward asked.

"Going on twelve," Ralph said.

"Likely you've run away," the steward said. "Come to my office and tell me your father's name. I'll send word that you are here."

But Ralph had turned and was running down the gangplank. The steward reached out to grab him by the collar, but Ralph was too fast for him.

Ralph didn't look back until he had gone a long way down the dock, past steamer after steamer. Only

when he was well down the line of boats did he stop
to look them over to choose the next one on which he
would ask for work.

They were all shapes and sizes. Most of them had
side paddle wheels, like the river steamers of the Ohio
and the Mississippi. But the lake boats were built for
deep water. They were much more graceful looking
than the riverboats. Most of them were only one-story
high instead of two, and they were more long and
slender in shape. Some were just for hauling freight.
Others were fine passenger steamers. Ralph did not
even think of working on a freighter. He chose the

best-looking passenger steamer at the far end of
the row.

"I wish to see the captain," he said as before.

But again he did not get past the steward. This
steward, too, asked many questions and Ralph hurried
away. On steamer after steamer, Ralph asked for work,
growing less and less sure of himself. Sometimes the
steward would only look at him and laugh. Other
stewards tried to be too helpful in returning him to
his family, as the first one had tried to do.

By one o'clock, there was only one passenger
steamer left to try. It had just tied up and unloaded

its passengers and freight. Ralph saw the name *Diamond* on its wheel boxes. Even he could see that it must have been a fine steamboat when it was new, although now it was old and shabby. By the time Ralph walked up the *Diamond's* gangplank, he had learned a little more about how to ask for work. He was hungry, too, and it was hard to act bold and fearless with an empty stomach.

He took off his cap and walked slowly up the gangplank. The steward himself stood leaning against the cabin wall. Ralph thought the steward looked a little like the steamboat—worn and old, but still strong. The man's mouth was set like one of the bolted steel arches that ran between the smokestacks over the hurricane deck. Ralph felt the steward's eyes upon him every foot of the way up the gangplank.

He stood before the steward and looked up into those eyes. They were cold and gray, like marbles. Ralph had the feeling they could see right into his mind.

"Please, sir, I would like to work on this steamer," Ralph said.

The steel-arch mouth and the see-through eyes didn't move as the steward grunted, "Hm-m-mph."

"Yes sir. I need work badly."

The steel arch bent a bit and the eyes were not cold gray marbles. Ralph was surprised at the softness of the steward's voice.

"What can a lad like you do? You ain't big enough to tote a bale on board, or even coil a line. We need a cabin boy, but you're much too small to carry heavy trays of dishes."

Ralph made himself as tall as he could. "I am much stronger than I look. I would make a good cabin boy, sir," he said.

But the steward was turning away. "Sorry, boy. I can't take a chance. The captain wouldn't like it if I hired a boy too small for the work. Once we're out on the lake, it will be too late to get a bigger boy. Better run along home."

Ralph's heart was sinking so fast it must surely hit his boot tops. This was his last chance, and the steward was about to round a corner and disappear. He ran after him.

"Please, sir!" he said. "I have no home to go to. I have no friends, and no one to help me. I *must* have work! Please, *please* let me try!"

Slowly the steward turned around. The steel-arch

mouth was set again, but Ralph thought he saw it twitch a bit. The gray marble eyes looked through him again.

"H-m-mph!" was all he said. He stood for a moment turning Ralph inside out with his eyes. Then he turned and walked away. Ralph could hardly believe the words that came back over his shoulder.

"Report to the pantry. You can help wash dishes."

Ralph's heart zoomed back up from his boot tops and pounded so hard in his chest that he put his hand over it to hold it in. He stood for a moment, trying to think where the pantry would be. Where had it been on the old *Indiana*? He chose the most likely route to the dining hall. He opened a door at the forward end. The stacks of dirty dishes on the tables inside the room told him he had found the pantry. This was the room where the serving dishes were filled and the dishes washed and stored.

A greasy-looking man leaned over an even greasier-looking pan of water on a table. Stacks of dirty dishes were beside the pan. But what took Ralph's eye was the table on which were platters of food left over from the meal served just before the steamer docked. There were slices of roast beef, turkey and ham. There was a bowl of gravy and enough left-over potatoes and bread for six boys. There was some spicy smelling pudding, too, and sauce to go over it. Ralph couldn't take his eyes from the food, even when the greasy man had dried his hands on his dirty apron and stood facing Ralph.

"Who are you?" the man asked.

Ralph's empty stomach answered for him.

"I came to get something to eat," he said.

The pantry-man's mouth hung open in surprise. But not for long. In a moment he had his hands on Ralph's shoulders and had turned him back toward the door. He was raising his foot to help push the boy out faster when Ralph cried, "The steward sent me!"

The foot lowered. "The *steward* sent you?" It was plain that he could see no reason why the steward should send the likes of this boy to his pantry.

"You can ask him if you want to," Ralph said. "He told me to come to the pantry."

The hands let go of Ralph's shoulders. The pantry-man shook his head and turned back to his dishpan. If the steward sent this lad, he must have had some reason. It was not for the pantry-man to ask the reason. He reached into the gray dishwater, pulled out the dishrag, and went back to work.

"There it is," he said, tipping his head toward the left-overs. "Pitch in."

Ralph loaded a plate with all it would hold. He was stuffing his mouth so busily a few minutes later that he did not see the steward standing in the pantry doorway. The steward had been standing there more than a minute when Ralph, reaching for a piece of bread to sop up gravy, chanced to see his boots.

His hand came back to his side without the bread. Slowly, Ralph raised his eyes from the boots upward, fearful of the anger that the "work" he was doing would bring onto his head.

Ralph's eyes reached the steward's face. The steel arch was not set, and the gray eyes weren't cold marbles.

"I-I-I'll get right to work," Ralph said, and he put down his plate.

The steward's voice was gentle. "Why didn't you say you were so hungry, boy?"

Ralph couldn't answer. He just looked down at the meat and gravy he hadn't finished and a tear fell onto the meat.

The steward cleared his throat. "There, there, boy.

Eat as much as you want."

The pantry-man said, "Tell him to hurry up about it and help me clean up these dishes to pay for all he's eaten."

The steward had been about to leave. He turned back, and his voice was sharp as he spoke to the pantry-man. "Let the boy alone. He's to eat all he wants."

He started out the door again, and again he turned back. This time he spoke to Ralph. "You needn't wash dishes. I'll let you try the work of cabin boy."

Nothing was said to Ralph then or later about pay for his work, and Ralph did not ask. It was enough for the moment to have a job on the steamer. The steward showed him what to do, and Ralph tried hard to please him.

When the passengers came on board the *Diamond,* Ralph helped carry their baggage. By this time, steamboats had staterooms for the passengers instead of just bunks in one large room, and part of Ralph's work was to see that they had everything they needed.

He was carrying a pitcher of water to one of the cabins when the boat began to rock badly. The water splashed over the top of the pitcher.

"Whoops!" he said, and tried to steady the pitcher.

The boat rocked more and more. He got most of the water safely to the cabin and then went on deck. He could hear the engines working and the steam hissing. The gangplank was pulled in. With a great clanking, the paddle wheels began to turn, and the boat backed clear of the dock.

The rocking was worse as the boat headed westward out into the open lake. Ralph was holding onto the railing when the steward came along.

"Are you a good sailor, Ralph?" he asked.

Ralph nodded and smiled. "Yes sir." He remembered the pleasant journey he had made from Toledo to Buffalo on the *Indiana*.

The steward said, "That's good, because this is going to be a rough trip. Strong wind from the northwest has old Lake Erie about as choppy as I've ever seen her."

Lake Erie is not as deep as some of the other Great Lakes. When it is quiet, it becomes quite smooth, like a smaller lake. But it can become rough very suddenly. Ralph could see the white caps all over the lake, and the choppy waves were setting the *Diamond* to rolling badly. As she nosed farther away from the dock out onto the open lake, the motion became worse.

It was about two hours later that Ralph became very sorry he had eaten so much food. By the time he should have been serving supper to the passengers in the dining room, Ralph was too sick to do anything but lean over the rail. The steward felt sorry for him and told him he could go to his bunk and not work any more that day.

It was that way all the way to Cleveland. Ralph was able to do some of his work of setting, clearing and waiting on tables and cleaning cabins, but the steward did much of it himself.

"What's wrong with that new cabin boy, Steward?" the captain asked.

The steward said, "He's a mite under the weather, sir, but he'll soon be all right. I'll see that he makes up for it when he gets his sea legs."

The Captain grunted and said, "Get rid of him if he's not a good sailor."

At last the boat docked at Cleveland. The steward looked into the dark little cabin where Ralph was lying on his bunk. Ralph had hurried back to it as soon as he'd finished carrying passengers' bags ashore.

"Want to go ashore for a bit, Ralph?" the steward asked. "We'll be tied up here for several hours."

Ralph got to his feet. Land! How good it would feel to have something steady under his feet!

"Yes, sir," he said. "Thank you. I'll come back when the *Diamond* is getting up steam."

It felt good to step onto the pavement. Ralph started up a street that led away from the choppy lake.

"Maybe if I can't see the water I'll feel better," he thought.

He looked into the shop windows and listened to the rough talk of the men who leaned against the old water front buildings. Slowly he walked up one block and then turned a corner.

"I'm beginning to feel better," he decided.

He found himself in a narrow street lined with little shops that sold things that sailors on shore leave might want. There was an interesting store near the corner. It had the biggest collection of second-hand junk that Ralph had ever seen. The dirty window was piled so high with odds and ends that Ralph could not see past them into the store. He pressed his nose against the glass, trying to see if there were something he might want to buy.

"I'm a working man now, and I can spend some money if I choose to do so," he thought, fingering the five buttery pennies in his pocket.

He decided to go inside where he could see more easily. But as he reached the open doorway, the smell of the store hit him. It smelled like the dark hold under the deck of the *Diamond*—water-rotted, tarry and stale. He backed out of the shop and something dangling over his head caught his eye. He hadn't noticed it before, but now he saw a suit of sailor clothes hanging outside, above the doorway, flapping in the breeze. There was a narrow-banded sailor hat at the top, a sailor blouse with its wide collar lifted high, and a pair of bell-bottomed trousers puffed out with air for all the world as if a ghostly sailor were in them.

"Like the picture of Captain Kidd in that book," Ralph said aloud, and in his mind he was back aboard the *Diamond,* sitting in the rocking forecastle looking at a greasy paged book one of the sailors had.

The sailor suit went limp as the breeze died. Then, suddenly, it puffed out again and the ghostly sailor was dancing a hornpipe. At the same moment another wave of the stale air from the store hit Ralph. It was too much for him. He was as seasick as ever. He hurried back to the *Diamond* and crawled into his bunk to suffer alone.

During the night, as the *Diamond* began its slow journey back to Buffalo, Lake Erie grew calm. By the time the steamer stopped at the first of the small cities that lay between the two large lake ports, Ralph was feeling fine. He found the journey much as he remembered it on the *Indiana,* and he began to enjoy his work as a cabin boy.

"Guess I'm a good sailor after all," he decided. He saw the captain's eyes resting on him without the angry look of the first journey. At the end of the trip he signed up for a third journey.

But the steamer was hardly out of the Buffalo harbor when again Lake Erie began to roll like a bucking bronco. Ralph had to hurry to the rail again.

The captain saw him. "What's the matter with that landlubber cabin boy of yours, Steward?" he said angrily.

"I'm sorry, sir," said the steward. "I thought he would get over it by now."

"See that he works, sick or not," the captain said.

So Ralph staggered about, trying to work even though he could not eat and the world went 'round and 'round. Carrying the loaded trays to the dining cabin was hardest for him to do, for his knees seemed to fold under him and he was afraid he would spill everything.

The steamer had just left the dock at Erie, Pennsylvania, when it was time to serve dinner. The passengers took seats at the long table down the center of the dining room. The table was set with the silver and china, but the food had to be brought from the pantry. It was always in large serving dishes from which the passengers helped themselves.

Ralph picked up a heavy tray on which were platters of meat and a bowl of stewed chicken. His knees almost gave way as he went through the pantry doorway into the dining room, but he steadied himself against the door frame for a moment. Then he staggered towards the table. Standing behind some passengers, Ralph tried to lift a platter of sliced meat from the tray to put it on the table, but just as he did so the boat rolled mightily. The tray tipped, and the bowl of stewed chicken slipped off.

Ralph's eyes grew large with horror as he saw it fall into the lap of a lady passenger.

"Oh, madam!" he cried out. "I am so sorry!"

He expected her to scream at him in anger, but she did not. She stood up quietly as the steward hurried forward with a cloth to wipe the mess from her skirt. Ralph glanced at the end of the table, where the captain's place was set, as he hurried to get a mop and bucket. What luck! The captain had been delayed and was not in his place!

The chicken was cleaned up and the captain had not arrived. Ralph leaned against the door frame inside the pantry, trying to steady himself.

"Get back to work, boy," growled the greasy pantryman. "Go in and see if the passengers need anything."

Ralph eased himself around the corner into the dining room. The captain was seated now, helping himself to food.

"Boy!" the captain called.

"He must have heard about the chicken," Ralph thought, and his heart sank. His feet seemed to belong to someone else as he made his way across the sea of flowered carpet that lay between the doorway and the captain's chair. It was almost too much for Ralph, and he fastened his eyes to the bald spot on the captain's head. If he did that, he was almost steady, and he kept his eyes on it as he stood before the captain.

"What are you staring at?" the captain asked,

crossly. But he didn't wait for an answer. "Get me a glass of water," he added.

Relief came over Ralph. He didn't know about the chicken! Carefully, he headed himself toward the sideboard where the water pitcher was. He picked it up, turned about, found the bald spot again, and set his course back to the captain.

He was so dizzy that he could hardly see where the water glass was. He found it, tipped the pitcher and started to pour just as the boat rolled more than usual. The stream of water poured out and Ralph had the horrible feeling he was aiming it at that steadying bald spot instead of the glass.

The captain jumped to his feet, water running over his ear, under his collar and down the sleeve of his uniform.

"What in blazes do you think you're doing?" he yelled.

Ralph dropped the water pitcher to the floor. The captain's roar, the shattering of glass and the spreading pool of water were too much to face. The boy ran for his bunk. He pulled the pillow over his head and tried to disappear.

The steward found him there. As gently as he could,

he delivered the captain's message. Ralph was to leave the *Diamond* at the next stop and never set foot on board again. At the moment it sounded fine to Ralph, and it was only when he had spent his five buttery pennies much later that he realized he had been given no pay for his trips as cabin boy.

Ralph was not a quitter. In time, he was working again on a lake steamer. But even though he got over his seasickness, he never became a captain. He decided that Lake Erie was too hard a master and he'd never make a fortune on a lake steamboat.

But never again did he work without knowing what his wages would be. He saved his money, and when he had enough he went back to school. In time, he became a writer and wrote the story of Lake Erie and the cabin boy.

SAM CLEMENS, CUB PILOT

It was the hey-day of the steamboats in the ten years before the War Between the States. Up and down the Ohio, the Mississippi and most of the Missouri River, the boats kept the water churning around their big paddle wheels. Smaller stern-wheel boats nosed up every smaller river with enough water to float the boats. Railroads were beginning to take over the work of the slow-moving canalboats, but the steamboats were still the main carriers of people and goods wherever the rivers and lakes reached.

While Ralph Keeler struggled with the heavy trays on the steamer *Diamond,* another boy about his age spent many hours on the banks of the Mississippi River a few hundred miles to the west, in the little town of Hannibal, Missouri.

The boy loved to hear the whistle of the steamboats and the calls of the rivermen as they went about their work. Especially, he loved to listen to the leadsmen, the men who stood at the prow of the steamboats measuring the depth of the water. As the leadsman saw that the steamboat was heading into water which might not be deep enough for the boat, he would drop a lead weight on a cord over the side of the steamboat. The cord was marked off at certain points, and the leadsman could read how deep the water was when the lead weight touched bottom.

"Mark three! Ma-ark three-ee!" he would call. Then, "Quarter-less-three!" Less of the string would be in the water as he called out, "Half-twain!" The words would float back to the shore where the boy listened, and they were a song in his ears.

He knew what was coming as the pilot nosed the steamboat carefully ahead, trying to pick a safe pathway between sandbars.

Came then the call the boy loved best. "Mark twain! Oh, Ma-ark twa-ain!"

"Mark twain" meant that the water was two fathoms deep, about twelve feet. This was deep enough to float almost any Mississippi River steamboat in the 1850's and there was a note of gladness in the leadsman's voice as he sang out again and again, "Ma-ark twa-ain! Oh, mark twai-ain-n-n!" as the water held to the needed depth.

The boy's name was Sam Clemens. When he began

writing things that were printed in the newspapers and then in books, such as TOM SAWYER, many years later, he still remembered that old call of "Mark twain," and Mark Twain was the name he chose to use as an author.

But the days of Mark Twain were to come much later. Young Sam Clemens dreamed, not of being a writer, but of being the man who was the true master of a steamboat—the pilot. His eyes always left the leadsman soon to look to the highest cabin on the big steamboat. It was called the pilot house, and in it, hands on the big wheel and eyes on the river ahead was the great man himself, the pilot. It was he who gave the orders, even to the captain, and it was his skill that took the river giant safely up and down the ever-changing river.

"Someday I'll be a pilot," Sam said, and his friends always chimed in with, "Me, too!" It was the dream of every Hannibal boy to ride the river as a steamboat-man, and best of all would be to be a pilot.

When one of the boys of Hannibal ran away from home and got work on a steamboat, he became a hero to the other boys. When his boat puffed into the dock at Hannibal, the boy made sure that he had work to do in plain sight on the deck where the stay-at-home boys could see him and envy him. When there was time to go ashore, he talked "steamboat talk" and told about the places he had been.

It was too much for many of the boys. All of them wanted to get work on a steamboat, and some of them did. Sam was one of those who wanted to go, but his family was against it. When Sam was in his teens, he learned the work of a printer, helping his older brother publish a newspaper. But when he was eighteen, Sam's old dream of being a pilot came back.

He tried to get work on a steamboat but had no luck. Then one day his luck changed. He was walking along with his head down because he felt so gloomy. A cold November wind was blowing and Sam was thinking how interesting it would be to be an explorer, especially in the warm country of the Amazon River in South America. He had been reading in the newspaper about an exploring party that was just starting out. But he forgot the explorers when a bit of paper blew against his trouser leg and held there until he got hold of it. It was a fifty dollar bill!

No one answered the ad he put in the paper about finding the money. Here was his chance! He bought a ticket on the steamboat *Paul Jones* and headed down the Mississippi to New Orleans.

On the steamboat, Sam listened to the talk of the crew and the old dream of being a pilot grew stronger each hour. He made friends with the mate and was allowed to sit in the pilot house and watch the pilot at work. As he watched, he wished he could know the feel of the wheel in his hands. What power there would be in guiding this giant of a steamboat around sand bars, snags and sawyers, and steering it within an inch of a dock! What fun to bark orders down the speaking tube and know that men three decks below would instantly follow them!

"Want to take the wheel a bit?"

Sam looked about. But there was no one in the pilot house but Pilot Horace Bixby and himself. Mr. Bixby must be speaking to him, Sam Clemens, just as if he could read his mind. Sam jumped to his feet and for the first time in his life steered a Mississippi River steamboat.

Down at New Orleans, Sam learned that there would be no boat going to the Amazon for quite a spell, but the idea of being an explorer had been pushed back to second place in Sam's mind. He went back on board the *Paul Jones* to call on Mr. Bixby.

"Mr. Bixby, you need a cub pilot," he told the older man in a sure voice. "It would help you a lot. A cub could take the wheel for you and let you rest."

Mr. Bixby said, "Is that so?"

"Yes, sir," said Sam.

"So?" Mr. Bixby's voice gave no sign that he understood what Sam wanted.

"How about me?" Sam said then, with some of the sureness gone from his voice.

Mr. Bixby pretended to be very surprised.

"*You?* Boy, it takes a real man to be a pilot!"

It took Sam three days to sell Mr. Bixby on the idea of taking him on. When a pilot took on a "cub," it meant that he would teach him enough so that the cub could become a pilot himself, able to handle a steamboat on his own.

"Cost you $500," Mr. Bixby told Sam at last.

This stopped Sam for a bit. He had only ten dollars.

"Of course, you'll only need $100 right away," Mr. Bixby added. "The other four hundred you can pay me when you are a working pilot."

Sam was sure he could get the $100 from his married sister in St. Louis, and when the *Paul Jones* pulled out of New Orleans, he was right beside Mr. Bixby in the pilot house.

Sam felt very important as he looked down at the other boats docked at New Orleans. He watched as Mr. Bixby straightened the *Paul Jones* around and started her up the stream. They went past the sterns of other steamboats so close that Sam was sure they were going to rub against them.

There were still several boats to pass when Mr. Bixby said, "Here, take the wheel. Shave those steamships as close as you'd peel an apple."

Sam's heart jumped. He swallowed hard and reached out for the wheel. He had to, for Mr. Bixby already had let go. He swung the wheel to turn the boat away from one that seemed right in the *Paul Jones'* path. He missed the other boat with plenty of water between them and found himself heading into the side of a steamboat coming downriver. A quick turn of the wheel back to the right, and the *Paul Jones* swung back again in time.

"Thank goodness I missed them," he was thinking when he felt Mr. Bixby take the wheel into his own hands.

"I told you to shave them!" the pilot said. "What

kind of a pilot are you? Are you a coward?"

The words cut Sam like a whip. Mr. Bixby cut so close to the next steamboats that it looked as if the boat must surely be wrecked. Then, with just a twist of his wrist, he would turn just enough to clear the other steamboats.

"Got to hug the bank, boy," he said. "The easy water is near the bank. The current is out a little way. When we are heading downstream, we want the help of the current. But going upstream, there is no use wasting steam power pushing against it."

"Oh, I see," said Sam. What had seemed like a dangerous game now made sense to him. Laughing, he said, "I'll take the downstream trips and leave the upstream to others."

Mr. Bixby did not laugh.

"Six-Mile Point," he said after a while, nodding towards the bank. Sam said nothing.

Later, he broke the silence with, "Nine-Mile Point."

Sam looked out the window at the place the steamboat was passing. Pleasant enough, he thought, but not particularly interesting.

The boat churned and pushed its way up the wide river.

"This is Twelve-Mile Point," said Mr. Bixby.

"Looks just like Nine-Mile Point," thought Sam. But he said nothing.

Mr. Bixby edged the boat around a bend, going very close to a point of land.

"The slack water ends here," he said. "See that bunch of China-trees? Now we cross over."

Without a wasted motion, he swung the big steamboat out into the river and cut towards the other bank. All the water looked the same to Sam.

It went on that way until the end of Mr. Bixby's watch at eight o'clock. Sam was given the wheel a time or two more, but only for a few seconds. He either came near chopping the edge off the land, or he took the boat too far from shore.

"You'll never make a pilot," said Mr. Bixby again and again as he snatched the wheel.

At the end of the watch, Sam ate his first meal with the steamboat crew. He felt quite important as he climbed into a crewman's bunk instead of heading for a stateroom at bedtime. But it seemed he had just closed his eyes when he felt a light shining on them.

"Come, turn out!" said the boatman with the light. Sam grunted and the man went on.

"Why should I get up now?" Sam thought. "It's the middle of the night!"

He turned over and went back to sleep. He was just comfortable when a rough hand was on his shoulder.

"Hey, you! I told you to turn out!"

Sam sat up. "Why do you want to come bothering around here in the middle of the night?" he asked, crossly. "Now, like as not, I won't be able to go back to sleep."

"Well, I'll be blessed!" said the watchman. "So you might not be able to go back to sleep!" and his voice imitated Sam's tones.

Other men were moving about in the cabin and they laughed loudly.

"Did you go and wake up the new little cub?" one of them said. "He needs his sleep! Maybe you'd better get some sugarwater for him and sing *Rock-a-bye Baby*!"

The laughs grew louder. Sam, wide awake now, felt his ears burning.

"Come on, boy, your watch is half over," the boatman said and moved on.

Sam was on his feet, luckily, when Mr. Bixby came in.

"Why aren't you up in the pilot house?" he roared.

All the way up the stairs, Sam tried to close his ears to the angry words of the pilot behind him. It just had never entered his head when he was a passenger on the *Paul Jones* that half the crew got up in the middle of the night to keep the steamboat moving on up the Mississippi.

The mate was holding the wheel. The only thing Sam could see that was guiding him in his steering was a star that was low in the sky. The *Paul Jones* seemed to be heading right towards that star. All else was blackness. Sam peered to both sides, but he could not see either shoreline.

"We've got to land at Jones' plantation, Mr. Bixby," the mate said as he turned over the wheel.

"He'll never find it in the dark of night," Sam thought. He would enjoy hearing Mr. Bixby say there was something he could not do.

But Mr. Bixby just said, "Upper end of the plantation or the lower?"

"Upper," said the mate.

Sam wondered how Bixby could even know where

the plantation was, let alone choosing one end of it. He was not surprised to hear Mr. Bixby say, "Can't do it!"

"Aha!" thought Sam. "Something he can't do, at last!"

But Mr. Bixby went on. "The stumps are out of water at this stage at the upper end. Mr. Jones will have to get along with our stopping at the lower end."

"All right, sir," said the mate as he left.

Mr. Bixby was steering towards the black shore just as if he could see where he was going. What was more, he was singing as he did so. Then his song stopped. Suddenly he turned to Sam.

"What's the name of the first point above New Orleans?" he asked.

Sam laughed, "I don't know, sir. What is it?"

"Don't know!" bellowed Mr. Bixby.

"No, sir," said Sam. He couldn't understand why this should be so disturbing to the pilot.

*"Well—*you *are* a smart one!" said Mr. Bixby. "What's the name of the *next* point?"

Sam began to feel a little frightened. "I—I don't know, sir."

"Well, this beats anything," said Mr. Bixby. "Tell

me the name of *any* point or place I told you."

Sam's mind went completely blank. "I can't, sir," was all the answer he had.

Mr. Bixby's neck was beet red. Sam was afraid he would actually blow up before he finally took a deep breath.

When he spoke again, his voice was held to an even tone. "Now, boy, think hard. What do you start out from, above the Twelve-Mile Point, to cross over?"

Sam swallowed hard. "I—I don't know, sir."

"You—you don't know, sir." Mr. Bixby's voice was weak, like Sam's. Then suddenly it changed to a roar. "Well, what *do* you know?"

"I—I—I—" Sam swallowed and tried a new start. "Nothing for sure, sir."

That was all Mr. Bixby needed.

"By thunder, I believe you!" he shouted, and Sam was sure every passenger in the staterooms on the second deck of the *Paul Jones* must be sitting up in bed listening. "Of all the stupid, empty-headed—why, you're the worst I ever heard of! What makes you think you can learn to be a pilot? You couldn't pilot a cow down a lane!"

He was too angry to say more.

When at last he could control his voice, Mr. Bixby said, "Look here, boy! Why do you suppose I told you the names of those points?"

"Well," Sam said in a voice as small as he felt, "to be—to be entertaining, I thought."

This was like holding a red rag in front of a bull. Mr. Bixby stormed and raged. He was so angry that he ran over the steering oar of a flatboat as he crossed the river again. He put his head out of the window and took out his anger on the poor flatboatmen. He went on yelling and talking long after the flatboat was too far away for the men to hear. Then at last, emptied of anger like a balloon from which all the air is gone, he stood quietly at the wheel.

There was silence in the pilot house for a long time. Then he spoke in a calm tone. "My boy, you must get a little notebook. Write down everything I tell you about the river. You have twelve or thirteen hundred miles of this river to learn. You have to know it by heart, as well as you know your A, B, Cs."

This was something new to Sam. He had never thought of the work it took to learn to be a pilot. It looked so easy, just to steer the boat along while everyone else on the steamboat did as you ordered.

As Mr. Bixby talked, he pulled a rope which rang a big bell. Sam looked out the window. Even the stars were gone now. There was nothing but blackness. But Mr. Bixby was bringing the boat to a stop at some unknown, black dock.

"Lower end of Jones' plantation," he said into the speaking tube. Boatmen on the main deck were tying the *Paul Jones* to the small dock.

Sam still could not believe that Mr. Bixby could find this one little landing on so black a night. But he heard a porter below call out, "Over here, Mr. Jones! I'll take your bag."

From then on, Sam did as Mr. Bixby said. Each day he wondered more and more at how well the pilot knew the river.

When at last he could "shave the boats" and "read the river like a book," Mr. Bixby said, "In spite of everything, you made it, son. You don't need me anymore. You're on your own."

THE CUB TAKES OVER

The sound of the ship's bell and the hoot of the whistle cut through the winter air as the *A. B. Chambers* backed off from the long levee at St. Louis. Up in the pilot house, Pilot Sam Clemens steered her easily down the Mississippi, "shaving" the long, long line of steamboats tied at the river's edge.

The mate and the captain of the *A. B. Chambers* stood on the main deck near the prow, looking out over the Mississippi River. Caked and frozen mud showed where usually the waters reached. A sand bar lay entirely uncovered that almost always was under several feet of water.

"Just doesn't look right to see the Mississippi River so low," Captain Bowman said. "When it gets too low for the Mississippi steamboats to pick their way through it even with good pilots like Sam Clemens, Old Man River is too low for much good."

"That's when Missouri River steamboats have to take over," said the mate. His name was Grant Marsh, and the Missouri River was where he had spent most of his time. Usually, the *A. B. Chambers* and other steamboats like her that were built for fighting the strong currents and sometimes shallow waters of the Missouri River, stood at the St. Louis levee all winter, waiting for the ice to melt upriver. But this year, the water was so low on the Mississippi that the big Mississippi steamboats couldn't travel. The Missouri River steamboats were being used to handle the Mississippi trade south to New Orleans.

Up in the pilot house, Sam Clemens steered the *A. B. Chambers* through the channel as it cut from one side of the river to the other. Mr. Bixby had taught him well. Piloting this small stern-wheeler was like handling a toy ship after guiding the giant Mississippi River boats. But there was one thing that bothered him. There were masses of ice chunks coming down the river from the north, jamming the channel sometimes so that it could be dangerous to try to get through. And the temperature was falling fast. There would be more and more ice if the cold snap did not break.

He spoke into the tube. "Send the leadsman ahead in the yawl." Then he signalled the engine room to hold down speed. It would be a slow trip, but he would do his best to take the *A. B. Chambers* safely to New Orleans.

The next afternoon it was colder than ever. Sam and the second pilot had so far kept the steamboat moving without hitting the great sharp chunks of ice that were piling ever higher. The second pilot was on duty when suddenly there was a scraping sound on the steamboat's hull. Bells rang and the paddle wheels were stopped.

"We're aground!" came the call. The passengers hurried from the cabins.

"Are we going to sink?" cried a lady.

"No, ma'am," said Captain Bowman, "but we are stuck. We'll try back-watering."

Soon the paddle wheels were turned to back the boat. They ground and churned the water, but the steamboat did not back an inch.

"Forward!" called the engineer. Sometimes they could dig a hole with the paddle wheels and get enough water to let the wheels have power enough to push the boat afloat.

But turning the paddle wheels backward and forward did not help this time.

"Try the spars!" called the captain. "We'll try

grasshoppering over the sand bar."

The passengers watched until they were too cold to stay outside any longer. They saw the men start up the small steam engine that was on the forward deck of every good Missouri River boat. While it was getting up steam, the two long poles, called *spars,* were hooked to ropes and pulleys and lowered into the water. When they were in the water, they looked like long grasshopper legs on the steamboat.

The small steam engine turned a big spool-like thing called a capstan. Rope wound around the turning capstan, pulling the whole steamboat up off the river bottom and forward, so that it was hung from the poles. Carefully, the boat was lowered and the spars moved forward. Again and again, the steam engine puffed, the ropes wound tighter, and the boat moved forward a little farther.

The sand bar was almost cleared when the engineer called to the captain, "Sir, we are out of fuel!"

The *A. B. Chambers* had planned to take on wood at a stop not far down the river from the sand bar. But the greedy little capstan steam engine had eaten up so much wood that there was not enough to rebuild the fires to get up steam for the big engines. Much fuel

had been wasted in trying to back-water off the sand bar. The steamboat couldn't even float slowly ahead to the next woodyard, for it wasn't yet clear of the sand bar.

Sam Clemens, off duty at the time, had been on the deck helping as he could. Captain Bowman spoke to him now.

"Sam, do you think you and Grant and a few of the boys could take the yawl upriver as far as Commerce? I remember seeing a wood-barge there. I want to have it floated down here."

Sam looked up the river. It was almost closed with floating chunks of ice. He knew that the *A. B. Chambers* was about two miles down the river from the town of Commerce, Missouri. It would not only be hard work rowing the small boat up the river, but it would also be dangerous. One big chunk of ice, coming down fast with the current, could break the yawl in two.

But he answered in his usual quiet voice. "Yes, sir. I can't see that there is anything else we can do. The passengers and the livestock on the boat will freeze to death if we can't get some wood to get up steam again."

"Fine," said Captain Bowman. "Grant, pick enough men to man the yawl. You had better get started right away."

Sam Clemens waited as the yawl was lowered into the dark water. The wind whipped sharply down the river, and he turned up his collar against it. "It must be well below zero and still getting colder," he thought. The six crewmen and Mate Grant Marsh were in the boat. It was his turn to jump down. In a moment he was seated at the yawl's stern, his hand gripping the rudder handle.

"All set!" Grant called from the bow, and the six men pulled at the oars. The yawl moved slowly away from the steamboat, fighting the wind and the current each inch of the way.

"We'll pull over to the Illinois shore," Sam said, and swung the rudder around.

Grant Marsh looked surprised. "Commerce is on the Missouri side, Sam. Why go all the way over to the Illinois shore?"

Sam had to shout against the wind to make himself heard.

"We'll save time in the long run—easier to pull close to the shore, and it is free of ice jams over there."

The men worked hard to cross the river with the current trying to force them downstream. But when they were near shore, the going was much easier. They needed their strength for rowing, and no one said much for about a mile. Then, as a long dark shape in the river came into sight, Sam called out, "Burnham's Island. We'll take the cut-off between it and the Illinois shore."

Grant looked a little puzzled, for he knew that Commerce was just opposite the island. By going on the Illinois side, they would go farther north than they needed to. Then he saw the reason for Sam's choice. The river between the island and Commerce was alive with ice jams. It would be far easier to reach the dock safely from up the river than fighting against the fast moving ice jams.

They reached the north end of the island.

"Now, boys," Sam said, "we'll have to be on guard in crossing over to the Commerce dock. You can see that the river is not very wide here because there are bluffs on both shores just above us. But that means the current is stronger. Most of the ice jams are following the channel on the other side of the island.

That is why we went the long way around. But be ready for anything now!"

They were around the end of the island when Grant pointed to a great pile of ice caught in the narrows of the river. It seemed to be growing larger even as he looked at it.

"Sam, look!" he yelled.

Sam was already studying the ice pile, trying to judge how much time there would be before a great mass of it would break off and come rushing toward them.

"Hold it here, boys!" he called out, and the men kept the yawl close in to the island's edge.

"If that ice lets go, it will catch us for sure," Grant said. "Hadn't we better get started while we can?"

"No," Sam said. "Wait. But be ready to start across when I give the signal."

For some moments they sat there. The yawl rocked on the water, but the men held it in place by back-watering with the oars.

Sam watched the movement of ice and water. The yawl would have to cut across the open water at a time when it would not be in the path of a large chunk of ice. If one of those ice cakes struck it, the boat would surely turn over. There was little chance of the crew swimming to safety, for none of them could fight a rush of ice.

As he watched, a great piece broke loose with a loud crack. Like a live thing it hurtled down the river, ahead of them.

"Now!" he yelled. The six oarsmen bent to the oars. Sam held tight to the rudder handle, angling the boat toward the Missouri shore. Grant Marsh kept a watch on the main ice pile.

Suddenly, the pile cracked open. With a roar, a mass of ice broke loose. The yawl was a few yards out from the island.

"Sam, turn back! We'll all be killed!" Grant cried.

The men at the oars stopped in the middle of a pull.

"No!" yelled Sam. "Pull ahead full speed. Pull! Pull as hard as you can!"

Grant Marsh closed his eyes and gripped the prow of the yawl. He heard the rushing of the ice. Sam must be crazy! Grant waited for the crash that would send them all into the black water.

He heard the urging in Sam's voice, "Pull------pull ------pull!" and at each "pull" the boat leaped onward.

The roar of the moving ice grew louder, drowning

out Sam's voice. At the sound of ice touching the boat's sides, Grant opened his eyes. The rhythm of the rowing was broken, but the way seemed to be opening before the little boat. The water was almost all clear to the Missouri shore. He turned and looked back over Sam Clemens' head.

There the ice had closed all the space through which they had come. Rough, tumbling ice chunks rushed between the little boat and the shore of Burnham's Island, roaring and groaning their way along.

As the men pulled to the shore, none of them felt the cold. Their brows were wet with sweat.

Grant Marsh ran his sleeve over his brow. "Thank goodness we had you along to pilot us, Sam," he said. "We would all be under that ice right now if I'd been giving the orders."

Sam grinned. "You learn to know every whim of this old river when you're a cub under Horace Bixby," he said. "You have to 'shave them close and read the river like a book!' "

RACE OF THE LEE
AND THE NATCHEZ

Sam Clemens' days on the Mississippi River ended as the War Between the States began. The steamboats went to war then, carrying soldiers and guns, food and ammunition to the battlefields. They were helped in this work by the Iron Horse, that could hustle the men and goods faster than the steamboat could, wherever tracks had been laid.

The old steamboatmen shook their heads as they saw the railroad taking over more and more of the steamboat's work. "Looks as if the Iron Horse is going to put the steamboat out of work," they said.

After the war, hundreds and hundreds of men swung picks and mallets, building miles and miles of railroad. More and more, the throaty hoots of the steamboat whistles were answered by the mocking "Whoo-oo!" of the Iron Horse as it carried goods and men where steamboats couldn't go.

By 1870 the steamboat's day of glory was over. The rivers and lakes were no longer the main highways of the United States of America. But that was the year of the steamboat race on the Mississippi River that has never been forgotten. Like a very special skyrocket at the end of a long Fourth of July celebration, the race of the *Natchez* and the *Robert E. Lee* brought the steamboat age to a glorious finish.

The excitement began as early as April.

"Have you heard about the big race? I'm betting on the *Natchez*."

"The *Natchez?* Fastest boat ever built," many people said.

Others said, "That *Natchez* is a fine steamboat, but the *Robert E. Lee* is better. The *Lee* will win."

Both steamboats were in the Mississippi River trade. Both were fine passenger ships, painted snow white with gold trim here and there. Their staterooms were furnished with only the finest of furniture. The carpeting in their great dining halls was of the thickest, and richest in color. From the ceilings hung great chandeliers, with hundreds of glass beads that sparkled like jewels.

The race was to be from New Orleans to St. Louis, beginning at five o'clock on the afternoon of June 30, 1870. People began to gather at the New Orleans water front hours before that time. The two steamboats stood at the dock, ready to go.

"Look at the *Robert E. Lee!*" people said over and over. "What has happened to her?"

The *Lee* did look strange, indeed. She had been stripped for action. Shutters, doors, deck furniture—everything not needed to make the boat go was gone. Where the deck was usually stacked high with freight, there was none. All the *Lee* carried was a supply of fast, hot-burning fuel to add to the coal fires for her furnaces. The people could see many barrels of the kind that people shipped bacon in in those days, and there were stacks of pine knots, sticky with resin. There were even boxes marked "Tallow Candles."

But the *Natchez* looked as she always did when it was time to begin a trip up the river. There were several tons of freight, and quite a few passengers were along the rails. There were not as many passengers as usual, because many people would not ride on a steamboat that was in a race. Too many of them had built up more steam pressure than they should have, and their boilers had burst. When that happened, the steamboat's days were ended, and so were those of most of the people on board.

The *Robert E. Lee's* whistle blared out. Steam

hissed and bells rang. Right at five o'clock, she began to back from the dock. She turned her paddle wheels to forward and started up the river just as the *Natchez* backed from the dock. She, too, set her nose upriver and her paddle wheels to churning the water. The big race was on.

"Just look at that beautiful steamboat," someone cried from the docks. He was pointing at the *Natchez*. "She cuts the water like a knife. Anyone can see she's built for speed. The *Lee* doesn't stand a ghost of a chance, even without a load!"

The *Lee* looked clumsy compared to the *Natchez*. It was a wider steamboat, and seemed to push its nose down into the water awkwardly, while the *Natchez* glided as gracefully as a swan.

Captain John Cannon, on board the *Robert E. Lee,* knew that he had a fine steamboat. But he also faced the fact that its lines were not built for speed.

"If I am going to win this race—and I intend to—I will have to do some planning," he had told his friends. Long before the race began, he had those plans all made.

In the dark of night, the most important of these plans was carried out. Another fast steamboat, the

Frank Pargoud, was getting up steam at the docks of the city of Baton Rouge, Louisiana. Her decks were loaded with tons and tons of soft coal, the kind of fuel steamboats were burning in their great furnaces by then.

It was one o'clock in the morning. The captain and the pilot of the *Frank Pargoud* watched from the pilot house, looking back down the river.

"Look at the sky," the captain said. It was a few minutes after one o'clock. "See that glow? That means just one thing—a steamboat coming full speed ahead with her stacks belching flame. It could be the *Lee.* Let's move out into the river."

Soon the whistled signal came, and the men on the *Frank Pargoud* cheered. It was the *Lee,* still ahead after six hours on the river. But not by much. The glow of a second steamboat already could be seen.

The *Pargoud* was moving along almost as fast as the *Lee* when the two ships were alongside each other. The *Lee* slowed down, but only long enough for the crews of the two steamboats to hook the *Pargoud* to the *Lee's* side. Then, as coal was moved from the deck of the *Pargoud* to the deck of the *Lee,* the engineers of each boat kept up a full head of steam.

Back on the *Natchez,* Captain Thomas Leathers gave the signal to slow down. He had a barge of coal waiting for him at Baton Rouge, and a crew ready to hook it on to the *Natchez* and unload it as quickly as possible. But even as fine a steamboat as the *Natchez* couldn't move fast towing a flat coal barge. The glow in the sky that marked the *Lee's* place moved farther and farther ahead.

"She'll burst her boilers," Captain Leathers said. "They are pushing too hard. The *Natchez* is the finer boat and we can still win. We are only ten minutes behind, and anything can happen."

All along the way, crowds watched and waited for the racers. It took a good steamboat about four days, running day and night, to make the trip up the Mississippi from New Orleans to St. Louis. The river was alive with boats of all kinds, too, filled with people who wanted the best view of the steamboats as they came by. At every city, the town cannons were loaded so that they could be fired when the leading racer arrived. Most places had a supply of fireworks ready, too.

Up at Memphis, Tennessee, the hotels were crowded. It was July 2, and a crowd of about two hundred people had come down from St. Louis to see the winning steamboat and follow it back to St. Louis. Word came that the racers would arrive in the night. Everyone in the city who was able to walk went down to the riverfront to see the excitement.

A little after ten o'clock there came the sound of a steamboat whistle from far down the river. It blew a long, loud blast.

"Here they come!" people shouted. There was a scurrying for the best places from which to see the river. Necks craned for the first sight of the boat when it should round the river bend.

"There's the winner!" Cheers broke loose.

A steamboat rounded the bend, its two tall smokestacks glowing from the heat of the fires that were working so hard to keep up full steam. The small running lights were the only other parts of the boat the people could see in the black of night until flashes of light showed where the small deck cannons were placed. The boom of the explosions reached the ears of the Memphis people.

"Boom! Boom!" answered the Memphis cannons.

The small boats on the river scurried to clear the way as the coming steamboat blasted out a throaty, "Toot—tooo-oot, toot-toot!"

She was almost up to the docks. As the cheers grew even louder, the Memphis city fathers decided the moment had come for full show of glory. Rockets rose to the sky and burst in a lovely flare of sparkling stars. Roman candles zoomed skyward. The steamboat tooted an answer once more.

Then she was in full view of the lighted landing. Eyes were strained to read the lettering on her side, just to make sure that the *Natchez* had not passed up the *Lee* since the last report.

"D-E-A-N."

Silence fell, and then an angry outcry arose. The steamboat *Dean* had played a trick on them all, acting as if she were the leading boat in the big race. All Memphis felt foolish. When the *Lee* did arrive, a little before midnight, there were no more fireworks. Even the powder for the cannons had been used up.

People who saw the *Lee* that night wondered if she could make it the rest of the way. Her smokestacks were glowing red, so hot were they from the fires of coal, pine resin and spoiled bacon.

But somehow she did, laboring and puffing, with the *Natchez* skimming along behind her. The bad luck came to the *Natchez* instead when she had to stop to repair a steam pipe near the end of the run. Fog came over the river and slowed her even more.

It was just after eleven o'clock in the morning of the biggest Fourth of July celebration St. Louis had ever had that the *Lee* came into sight. She had set a new record—three days, eighteen hours and fourteen minutes for the run of 1,278 miles. The time was engraved on a great, tall silver cup that was given to Captain Cannon. The poor *Natchez* didn't get to St. Louis until nearly six o'clock on that Fourth of July.

Some said the race wasn't fair because of the special things Captain Cannon had done to help the *Lee* win.

But the *Lee* backers said, "There were no rules against Captain Cannon using his head to help him win. The *Robert E. Lee* is the winner, fair and square!"

The judges agreed, for the names of the *Robert E. Lee* and Captain John W. Cannon were placed on the great silver cup. It can be seen today in an honored place in a museum in St. Louis. It is the symbol of the glorious finish to the days when the water highways carried the life blood of commerce in our growing nation.